THE RICHEST MAN IN TOWN

BY V.J. SMITH

Library of Congress Control Number: 2005926232
ISBN: 978-0-9908739-1-4

Cover Design: Hitch Design Studio, Brookings, SD

Artist drawing of Marty and V.J.: Mr. John Livingston, Brookings, SD

Printed in the United States of America

Comments and queries can be directed to:
Life's Great Moments
P.O. Box 742
Brookings, SD 57006
Website: www.vj-smith.com
Email: thankyou@brookings.net

Contents

Introduction

by V. J. Smith

     ∞   *I'm so glad I found you.*

My friend, Aaron "Marty" Martinson, wrote those words in a note to me. On the pages that follow, you will discover that he didn't find me. I found him. And, thanks to Marty, I remembered a few things about life that I hadn't really thought about for a long time.

For years I had grand visions of writing a book about a leader who changed the course of history. I filled my personal library with biographies of presidents and statesmen. I wanted to understand what made their lives great—and what might be missing from mine.

In looking for answers I turned to books written by people who are successful in business and industry. For a while I searched for excellence, then I compared my habits to those of highly effective people. More recently, I tried to figure out which mouse I was in the pursuit of cheese. Like millions of people, I thought success equaled happiness.

The book I've written, though, is about a simple man who ran a cash register. He worked hard and was good to people. That, in turn, made him happy.

Can it be so simple—so free of complications? Marty thought so. He showed me how to be a better person, not one wealthier or more successful or more powerful.

He changed my life—forever.

CHAPTER ONE
The Handshake

∞ It's amazing what can happen just by paying attention. Besides, I never thought I would have a life-changing experience at Wal-Mart.

I don't remember the exact date I met Marty for the first time. Up to that moment, nothing that day seemed particularly important—certainly not what brought me to the store in the first place. Like a lot of people who want to get through a checkout line, my thoughts were on speed, nothing more. The line I was standing in wasn't moving as quickly as I wanted, and I glanced toward the cashier.

There stood an affable-looking man in his seventies. Slightly stooped and of average build, he wore glasses and a nice smile. I thought, well, he's an old guy and it probably takes him a little longer to get the chores done.

For the next few minutes I watched him. He greeted every customer before he began scanning the items they were purchasing. Sure, his words were the usual, "How's it going?" But he did something different—he actually listened to people. Then he would respond to what they had said and engage them in brief conversation.

I thought it was odd, but I guess I had grown accustomed to people asking me how I was doing simply out of a robotic conversational habit. After a while, you don't give any thought to the question and just mumble something back. I could say, "I just found out I have six months to live," and someone would reply, "Have a great day!"

This old cashier had my attention. He seemed genuine about wanting to know how people were feeling. Meanwhile, the high-tech cash register rang up their purchases and he announced what they owed. Customers handed money to him, he punched the appropriate keys, the cash drawer popped open, and he counted out their change.

Then magic happened.

He placed the change in his left hand, walked around the counter to the customer, and extended his right hand in an act of friendship.

As their hands met, the old cashier looked the customers in the eyes.

"I sure want to thank you for shopping here today," he told them. "You have a great day. Bye-bye."

The looks on the faces of the customers were priceless. There were smiles and some sheepish grins. All had been touched by his simple gesture—and in a place they never expected.

Some customers would walk away, pause for a moment, and look back at the old cashier, now busy with the next customer. It was obvious they couldn't quite comprehend what had just happened. They would gather their things and walk out the door, smiling.

Now it was my turn. As expected, he asked me how I was doing. I told him I was having a good day.

"That's good," he said. "I'm having a good day, too." I glanced down at the name tag on his red vest, the kind experienced Wal-Mart cashiers wore. It read, "Marty."

I said, "It looks like you enjoy your job, Marty."

He replied, "I love my job."

Marty told me how much I owed and I handed him some money. The next thing I knew he was standing beside me, offering his right hand and holding my change in his left hand. His kind eyes locked onto mine. Smiling, and with a firm handshake, he said, "I sure want to thank you for shopping here today. Have a great day. Bye-bye."

At that moment I wanted to take him home and feed him cookies. It was as if Sam Walton had come back from the dead and invaded this old guy's body.

I left the store, walked through the parking lot and got into my car. On the drive home I couldn't shake what had just happened. I had been in that store a hundred times and had never walked away feeling like that.

Who *was* that guy?

He did something different—
he actually listened to people.

CHAPTER TWO
The Letter

∾   Like most people, I procrastinate. I get a thought, but then I don't act on it.

Many times I would see someone in our town doing something nice. On crisp autumn days I would see kids from local churches raking leaves for the elderly. On cold winter mornings I would stand in my warm living room and watch a neighbor firing up his snow blower to clear the sidewalks and driveways for neighbors who could no longer heft a shovel. I would think to myself, "I should write a letter and acknowledge that kind act." Time would pass and another letter—always well-intentioned—would go unwritten.

Kind acts are common in our town, just as they are in many small towns. Our town is Brookings, South Dakota. Visitors entering Brookings drive past a sign noting a population of more than eighteen thousand people. Added into that is another eleven thousand, the number of students who attend South Dakota State University, the state's largest college.

People trust each other in Brookings. Each summer, a local farmer rolls a flatbed trailer into town and sells corn. That in itself isn't unusual. What's different is that no one is there to take your money. People simply grab ears of corn, then stuff dollar bills into a metal box. The honor system still works in Brookings.

The tree-lined main street conjures up hometown images from old movies. Shopkeepers greet customers by name. Almost fifteen years ago, many of those business owners were uneasy and uncertain when Wal-Mart opened a store on the east edge of town. Wal-Mart openings often cause angst in communities, but they do bring jobs. Marty had one of them.

For several weeks after I first noticed Marty, I would find myself in his line at Wal-Mart. I marveled at how he treated people. He was quick to give compliments. "You have a beautiful smile," he would say. Or, "That's a great-looking coat." If he wasn't saying nice things, he would ask people questions. Marty was a master at making other people the center of attention.

There was something else I noticed. His line was always the longest in the store. Some of the other checkout counters would have no customers standing in line at all. There would be three or four people in Marty's line. People didn't seem to mind that they had to wait a few extra minutes. I later found out that he had the store's highest IPH—items per hour—in spite of the time he took with people.

Marty said, "I like to show 'em what an old man can do."

∞ Four of us were standing in Marty's line one day when a young cashier came up and said, "I can help you in my line." We simply shrugged our shoulders and declined her offer. Nothing personal, of course. We just wanted the Marty touch.

Every time I was in Marty's line I would think to myself, "Someone needs to write a letter to corporate headquarters and tell them about this guy." A little voice in the back of my head would reply, "You're someone—why don't you?"

I always had an excuse.

As alumni director at South Dakota State University, I traveled throughout the United States, attending events and fostering school spirit. There would be a lot of small talk, a lot of listening, and a lot of handshaking. Airports, rental cars, and hotel rooms were constants in my life.

Several years ago, I began receiving requests to do motivational and inspirational talks. I would spend countless hours driving on moon-lit nights and weekends giving speeches in distant places. It seemed like I was always getting oil changes or buying new tires for my car.

All those excuses vanished the day I found myself in Marty's line behind a young mother. She had a pair of little boys with her, probably two and four years old. The mother turned to me and pointed at Marty. "He's everybody's grandpa," she said. I smiled at the thought.

The line moved forward and Marty greeted the young mother and her boys. As the mother wrote a check, Marty talked to the boys. He gave them some peppermint candy he had pulled from his shirt pocket. He handed the woman her receipt and change, shook her hand, and thanked her for her purchase. Then, he bent down and hugged those two little boys. That family smiled a collective smile as they walked out the door.

Marty was in their heads.

I couldn't take it any more. After Marty was done with me I walked over to the service counter and asked to see the manager. A few moments later a young man walked up to me. "I'm the manager," he said. "How can I help you?"

I pointed in Marty's direction. "That man over there—what is his name?"

The manager said he couldn't tell me Marty's full name because it was against company policy. Not wanting to push it, I asked the manager if he could give me the name and address of the chief executive officer of Wal-Mart. He left and came back a few minutes later to hand to me a piece of paper with the head man's name and address.

I drove back to my campus office. Colleges are buildings filled with people thinking deep thoughts. My thoughts that day were on a cashier at Wal-Mart.

I sat at my desk and wrote a letter to Mr. David Glass, president and chief executive officer of Wal-Mart, Bentonville, Arkansas.

Dear Mr. Glass,

Sam Walton would be proud of Marty. To me and lots of other people he is "Mr. Wal-Mart."

Funny, I don't even know Marty's last name. But let me tell you what I do know about him. Marty works at Wal-Mart in Brookings, S.D. He is a kindly older gentleman with twinkling eyes and a ready smile.

I, like many others, will stand "eight deep" in his cashier line. There will be a few people in the other cashier lines, but that doesn't matter, we like Marty's line. The wait doesn't bother us. Why? Because after he rings up the sale, and just before handing us the change, he sticks out his right hand to shake ours. He looks us right in the eye and thanks us. And, he sincerely means it and we know it.

I do a lot of public speaking in the area. One of the customer service items I speak about is the importance of saying "thank you." Until this morning I did not know Marty's first name. But I always refer to him in my talks and people in the audience immediately know who I am talking about. It's amazing! All of us are willing to spend a little extra time because we love to hear him thank us.

As long as Marty's running a cash register I'm going to stand in his line no matter how long it is. Yup, Sam Walton would be proud.

Sincerely,

V.J. Smith

∞ Marty was in my head.

I put a stamp on the letter, pounded it one time with my fist to make sure it stuck, and smiled. This was a first for me. I had never written a letter to any business to praise one of its employees. The letter left in the morning mail.

That afternoon a young man dropped by my office. His name was Casey Estling. Casey was an all-conference basketball player on our university's basketball team. He was a good player and an excellent student.

Casey told me he had been asked to give the graduation speech at commencement exercises that spring. It was an honor—and a daunting task. You stand up in front of nine thousand people, perhaps quote a dead poet or two, and try to inspire the members of your graduating class while impressing their families and friends.

I asked Casey what he wanted to talk about. He said he needed to thank people who made a difference in his life while he was a college student. That seemed like a good idea, and I suggested Casey think about it over the weekend, compile some type of list, and come back the following Monday to talk about it.

When Casey returned to my office he announced, "I've got it!"

He plopped down in a chair across from my desk, pulled out a piece of paper, and read from it. The first words were, "There's this guy at Wal-Mart by the name of Marty."

My jaw dropped. I quickly went through my in-basket to find a copy of the letter I had sent to David Glass of Wal-Mart. I handed it to Casey. "Read this," I said.

After a moment or two Casey looked up at me. "Boy," he said, "he's having an impact on a lot of people's lives." We talked about it and Casey decided that Marty would be a central character in his graduation address—a store cashier held up as a positive example at a college graduation.

Marty was in his head, too.

Two weeks later, Casey was back in my office. He said Marty wanted to meet me.

"I went through his line yesterday," Casey told me. "He asked me if I knew you. Evidently that letter you sent has come back through the chain of command because they pulled all the employees together yesterday morning and read your letter. Everyone cheered for Marty. Now he wants to meet you."

I waited a week. To be honest, I didn't know how I was going to introduce myself. It seemed awkward if I just walked up to him while he was working and told him who I was. So, I hatched a plan.

I went to Wal-Mart and picked out a dozen golf balls and a bag of tees and placed them on the black conveyor belt that led to Marty. He greeted me as usual and rang up the purchases. He said, "That will be twenty-one sixteen."

I pulled out a personal check, my name and address printed in the corner. After writing the check I handed it to Marty. He took it, went to the cash register, and started punching in the numbers. He paused when he saw my name.

Marty looked toward me and glanced back at the name on the check. Then he stopped what he was doing, walked around the counter, and thrust his arms around me in a bear hug. I paused for a moment before I thought, "Oh, what the heck," and threw my arms around him.

Two guys hugging in Wal-Mart.

Marty pulled back and grinned. "I've sure wanted to meet you," he said.

I told him I wanted to meet him, too. We talked for a moment and then he asked if we could get together some night to talk over coffee. It seemed like a great idea. We set a time and place and I left the store.

I don't know which one of us was more excited at that moment. Of one thing I was certain—I was thrilled that I had finally taken time to write that letter. It turned out to be the best one I ever sent.

All had been touched by his simple gesture.

CHAPTER THREE
Coffee, Tears, and Fried Corn Meal Mush

∞ "You don't know what you've gotten yourself into," Marty said as I greeted him in the restaurant of a local grocery store. That's the place he picked for our first meeting.

Marty had been sitting in a booth drinking coffee when I arrived. I brought a notebook and pencil with me. This man had a story to tell and I felt a need to record it.

I had already been referring to Marty's customer-service qualities in my speeches, but other than the few moments I had seen him at Wal-Mart, I didn't know anything about him. Why was he so different than any other cashier I had ever met? I had no intention of writing a talk about his life, much less a book. I just wanted to know why he was so happy—and what I could learn from him.

After buying a cup of coffee I sat down with him. Idle conversation filled those next few minutes until I asked, "Are you married?"

Marty's eyes lit up. "I got married to the most beautiful girl in the world—and she still is. Her name is Mickey and you need to meet her." I told him I would like to do that.

"Kids?" I asked.

"Four," he said, "three boys and a girl."

I opened my notebook and asked Marty if it was okay to write down his answers to my questions. Marty looked at the notebook and grinned. "You want to write stuff about me?"

It was obvious he hadn't been interviewed before. I thought I'd start with some easy questions.

"When were you born?"

"August 12, 1926. I'll be seventy-four years old this August. It's hard to believe."

"So you had to go through the Great Depression. What was that like?" I asked.

He paused for a moment, looked at his hands circling the coffee cup, and let his mind take a trip back in time. "We just lived life from day to day. My family was very hard-up at that time and I just figured everyone else was in the same boat. Most of them were."

Marty's mother stayed at home to take care of him and his brother and two sisters. His father was a common laborer, moving from one job to the next, often taking the family from town to town. In one place he worked on a turkey farm, in another he tended bar. Maybe it was the times, mixed with his lack of any particular skill.

"Growing up in the thirties and forties, people cared about people," Marty said. "We helped each other out without giving it a second thought. I suppose that's carried over to today."

As a young boy Marty watched his father pour drinks at a bar. "I remember a lot of men who worked hard in the stone quarry and when they got their paychecks they would go to a beer parlor. They would squander their money while their family was at home with very little to eat. I guess that is one of the reasons why I never drank."

After taking a sip of coffee, Marty continued. "We were dirt poor. Most days I ate a piece of bread smeared with lard and sprinkled with some salt and pepper on it. I don't ever remember eating red meat during the entire thirties. I never got to go to a restaurant until I was ten years old."

He started to laugh. "Have you ever had fried corn meal mush?" I told him I had never heard of it. "I'll fix it for you sometime. I still eat it because I kind of like it," he said, still laughing. I was smiling, too, as he remembered those years.

"I'll tell you how bad it got," Marty told me. "When I was eight years old I had a pet chicken. She would follow me around like it was a dog. Usually you can't pick up a chicken and hold it, but that one you could. Things got so bad we were forced to eat the poor thing. I cried, but I had to eat. That's the way it was."

My smile quickly faded. Now I felt bad for smiling. These could be sad memories for Marty. Yet, he continued to share them with me.

"When I was a kid I went to the dump ground and found the inner tube of an old tire. I made myself a slingshot. I got good with that slingshot and, once in a while, I got a rabbit."

Marty was silent for a time, then tears ran from his eyes. In a quiet voice he said, "You know, one of the greatest memories I have of my mother was the day I walked through the front door holding two rabbits. My mother sat at the kitchen table and cried. She couldn't believe we had two rabbits to eat." His voice trailed off. We said nothing for a few minutes, just drank coffee and wiped away tears.

Finally, Marty said, "My problem is that I'm a softy. I got that from my mother. Can we talk about something else?"

At that point I scrambled for something to ask. The first six questions I had written on my list dealt with family matters. It was obvious I needed to change directions.

"Why do you shake hands with the customers?" I asked.

The question revived him. "It happened by accident," Marty replied. "A couple of years ago, when I was first hired as a greeter at the store, four college students walked in. I shook their hands. One guy walked a few steps, turned around and said, 'I like that!' So I've been doing it ever since.

"I shake hands with two hundred and twenty people a day. Some people want a hug. There was one lady who wanted a kiss." He laughed. "Most people seem to like it. I know some don't. Germs, you know. There was one guy who wouldn't shake my hand because, he said, 'I'm a Quaker, not a shaker.' I'm still trying to figure that one out."

He had given a lot of thought to the technique behind that hand-shake. "You have to look people dead in the eye when you shake their hand. That's the only way to go. I'm trying to show them that I appreciate them," he said.

The shaking of hands surprised the newcomers to the store. Most of the locals expected it, and liked it, but for the uninitiated, it was a whole new experience.

"Oh, let me tell you a story," Marty said. "A year ago a woman came through my line and I stuck out my hand. She jumped back. She acted like I had a gun or something. I said to her, 'Hasn't anyone ever shook your hand before?' The lady said, 'I'm from South Carolina. There's a store in South Carolina where they shake hands all the time.'

"I yelled, 'Hooray for South Carolina!' and she walked out the door. Five minutes later she was back in my line, buying nothing. I said, 'Can I help you?' She touched my arm and said, 'I lied to you. I got out in the parking lot and started thinking about it. There's no store in South Carolina where they shake hands. You're the first one. I needed to come back in here and apologize for lying. Will you accept my apology?'"

Marty whacked his hand on the table and laughed. "Do you believe that?" he asked.

I grinned and thought to myself, "Marty got that woman to find religion in the parking lot of Wal-Mart."

At that point a restaurant worker came by with a mop and a pail filled with water. It was a signal our conversation needed to come to an end. I told Marty I would like to talk to him again. "That would be great," he replied. "Why don't you come to my house next Tuesday night? You can meet Mickey."

"Where do you live?"

"Number Fifty-seven, Normandy Village," he said. I had to think for a moment before I remembered that Normandy Village was a trailer park. I had driven by there many times.

"Oh," I said, "you live in a trailer?"

Marty looked at me and with a quiet sense of pride said, "I own a double-wide."

We shook hands and said goodbye. I left the store with more questions than I had when I walked in. The main one was simple: Why was he so happy?

I had known a lot of people who owned big cars, earned big paychecks, lived in big houses and had seemingly perfect family lives. Yet they were miserable. This guy was still working into his seventies, came through some tough times and didn't seem to have a lot of material things. He was the happy one.

I was hoping to find my answers in a trailer park.

"You have to look people dead in the eye when you shake their hand."

CHAPTER FOUR
Nights at the Round Table

⚮ Narrow roads wound through the Normandy Village trailer park. Following Marty's directions, I made two quick lefts and suddenly found myself staring at a double-wide home. "That must be it," I thought.

Marty greeted me at the door with a brisk handshake. "Welcome. This is Mickey," he said. Mickey had kind eyes and a warm smile. She appeared to be a little shy, even when I extended my hand. After a few moments, Marty said, "Let's go into the kitchen and sit at the table."

That round wood table became our visiting place on countless nights. I would sit directly across from Marty. Mickey would be only an arm's length from her husband.

The coffee pot was always on. Several times during the course of an evening Marty or Mickey would ask, "Can I get you another cup of coffee?" Then, they would politely argue about who would get the cup. "I'll get it, honey, just sit down," or, "No, babe, I've got it." This happened time after time.

I don't like to drink coffee at night. Not wanting to offend them, I drank it anyway—and drank some more. Sometimes eight cups of coffee at a sitting. I found out later that Marty purposely kept my cup full, thinking I would leave if it were empty. It was his way of saying, "Please stay."

I brought along my notebook for my early visits to the Martinson home. On that first night, I opened it and Marty looked at Mickey. He nodded toward the notebook and said, "See, he writes stuff down."

∞ Marty left school in the ninth grade to earn money for the family. For the next three years he worked in a traveling carnival. The job required him to operate all the rides and run penny-pitch games and the dart booth. Marty said, "The people I worked with weren't regular carnies, they were clean people."

Life with the carnival ended with a draft letter from Uncle Sam in

August 1944. Marty was eighteen years old when the United States was fighting wars on two fronts. As a private in the United States Army, he sailed to the Philippines to fight the Japanese.

"I got shot at," Marty said, "and I shot back." He sent most of his pay home so his parents could buy a house.

Marty was part of what Tom Brokaw called "The Greatest Generation." I thought he might like to tell me about some of his experiences. I asked him, "Do you have special memories of the war?"

The question turned him silent. Tears filled his eyes, and in a soft voice he said, "I saw so many of my friends blown up in front of my face. I can't talk about it." So we didn't.

He could talk about the end of the war. He was on a troop transport ship anchored a few miles off the Japanese coast awaiting orders. "Our commander told us that a lot of us were going to die when we invaded Japan. I was scared to death," he said. Then atomic bombs destroyed the cities of Hiroshima and Nagasaki, forcing the surrender. Marty said, "When I heard about the bombs, I was happy. Now, I feel sad about those poor Japanese people who died. But I got to go home."

Other wartime memories were just too painful. His grandson asked him to come to school to talk about World War II. On the night he told me about his grandson's invitation he said, "I … I … I … *can't*." Then he threw back his head and let out a high-pitched cry.

Mickey jumped from her chair and put an arm around Marty. "It's okay, honey, it's okay," she told him. "You don't have to talk about it."

∽ Mickey had grown up under difficult circumstances, too. When she was nine years old, her parents were forced to give up their children because they couldn't care for them. Nine brothers and sisters were shipped off to orphanages.

Marty's quiet way attracted her when they first met. It also nearly kept them apart.

Mickey found the other men she had dated a little too brassy for her. She met Marty through her sister. "He was quiet, shy, and handsome," she told me. But Marty was too shy to ask her out, and she insisted that he personally ask her for a date. He had approached her sister to see if Mickey might be interested in him.

He did ask her out. Still uncertain whether she wanted to date him, Mickey asked her sister what she thought of Marty. "He would be a good catch," she said. "Besides, he's good to his mother."

That was enough. They courted for two years before they were married by a justice of the peace in a furniture store on June 1, 1950. "That was when you could get married for two dollars. The license cost us two bucks," Marty said.

"And we had to borrow that!" chimed in Mickey. They both laughed at the memory.

"We've had a beautiful marriage," Marty said. "Our friends call us the M&M kids. Get it? M for Marty and M for Mickey."

The early years were difficult ones for the M&M kids, as they were for most young couples they knew. "We brushed our teeth with Lifebuoy Soap," Marty said.

His wife worked as a store clerk for thirty-five cents an hour. "We paid a babysitter twenty-five cents an hour," Mickey said, "so I was working for eighty cents a day."

Their only guilty pleasure was smoking. That, too, was subject to their tight budget.

"We smoked Wings cigarettes," Marty told me. "You could get

'em for fifteen cents a pack. They were really long so we cut them in half. Instead of having twenty cigarettes, we had forty."

Marty worked in newspaper shops in a few small towns over the course of forty-two years before he retired. "It's my only regret. I should have quit sooner," he said. "I love mixing with people and I get to do that now."

He worked in a restaurant for a while, then for seventeen months took care of a man who suffered from Parkinson's disease. He worked for another restaurant after that.

Then a friend heard that Wal-Mart was looking for greeters at the local store, and he encouraged Marty to apply. The woman who hired Marty told me that when she offered him the job he broke down and cried.

I asked Marty about that moment. He said, "Yeah, I remember it. After she told me I was hired she walked out into the hallway and I heard her say to someone, 'Boy, I've got a honey in here.'"

CHAPTER FIVE
What Matters Most

∞ Companies invest a lot of money in trying to find ways to help their employees work smarter and faster. In my working lifetime, I have spent countless hours attending seminars designed to improve my job performance. Twice I attended a class on "how to get along with difficult people." But no one has ever sent me to a seminar on how to be a better person.

I doubt that Marty ever attended a training session on customer service. He didn't read self-improvement books, either. What he did do was try to be good to people.

During one of his performance reviews, his supervisor, following management's procedures on conducting such reviews, asked him, "Do you have any goals?"

"Yeah," Marty said. "My goal is to stay here long enough that you have to carry me out."

Marty loved his job. "I get all pumped up going to work," he told me one night at his kitchen table. "It energizes me. People do this to me. The way I've got it figured, in life you get what you give."

Night after night, sitting at Marty's kitchen table, I learned life lessons. That was the first: *Relationships matter most in life.*

∞ "What I give are smiles, handshakes, thank-you's and, once in a while, a hug. What I get back I can't describe. It makes me want to go to work in the morning."

Marty said, "See, people think I'm just doing this just for them. I'm doing it for me, too."

In his mind, it was a circular relationship. He told me he was committed to taking the first step.

"Getting people to smile makes my day," he said. He recalled an older woman who came through his line and never smiled. "I didn't quit trying to make her smile. On about the eighth time she finally broke. I knew I had to say something, so I said, 'You have a beautiful smile.' Now she smiles all the time. I'll be at my cash register and she's a few people back in line waving at me and saying, 'Hi, Marty!'"

He had a satisfied look on his face when he told that story. "I'm convinced even grumpy people will smile if you shake their hand."

Marty was the scourge of grumpy people. One day when I was in his line an older gentleman stood beside him talking about a pharmaceutical plan that he insisted Marty investigate. Marty was paying half-hearted attention to the man, realizing that customers were waiting in line. He didn't want to offend the guy, nor did he want the customers to wait. It was a dilemma for him.

A young couple in front of me, obviously new to Marty's line, was becoming more agitated with each minute. Finally, Marty was able to break away from the guy pushing the drug plan and greet the young couple.

"How are you doing?" he asked, but they didn't respond. I could see why—they were angry.

Marty was oblivious to all of this. While the young man wrote a check, Marty shook the young woman's hand and said some nice things to her. The expression on her face changed from anger to confusion to an all-out smile.

After the young man handed him the check, Marty shook the young man's hand and apologized for the delay. He told them, "Now you two go out and have a great day."

As the couple walked away from Marty, the man looked at the woman with disgust on his face. The woman smiled at him and said something. Soon, the man smiled back at her and simply shook his head. They laughed as they walked out the door.

They couldn't stay angry. Marty had disarmed them.

∞ In time, it seemed that everyone in town and the surrounding area was getting to know Marty. He couldn't go to a grocery store or walk down a street without someone yelling, "Hi, Marty!" If people didn't know his name, they would simply refer to him as "that cute old guy that shakes hands."

Mickey said, "We can't go anywhere anymore without someone recognizing him."

On a flight to California, Marty and Mickey had a layover in Denver. While they sat at the gate three different people came up to speak to him. One said, "How are they doing back at Wal-Mart without you?" Marty didn't recognize any of them.

I was having dinner with Marty and Mickey at a local Chinese restaurant when a woman walked by. She stopped, looked at Marty and exclaimed, "Oh, honey, I've missed you!"

Marty looked up from his plate of food, not knowing quite what to say. "Well," he said, "I've missed you, too!"

They talked for a few minutes. She said she had moved out of town the previous year and was back visiting old friends. "Oh, golly, I'm glad I got to see you again, Marty," she said before walking away.

I asked Marty who she was. He looked puzzled and said, "I don't have a clue."

Not remembering people's names frustrated Marty. But he greeted hundreds of people each day and accepted the fact that it was impossible for him to remember the name of everyone he met.

But people remembered Marty. They dropped off gifts for him at the store. During the summer months countless bags of fresh corn and tomatoes came from the gardens of customers. Zucchini season nearly killed him.

✎ On a September day, I was in Marty's line and he said, "I was hoping you would come by today. I've got something to show you."

He reached into the pocket of his red vest and pulled out a white envelope containing a card. "This came attached to a jar of crabapple jelly," Marty said. "A young woman dropped it off yesterday, but I wasn't here. I got it this morning. Read it."

The woman wrote: "The last time I was in the store I asked you what your secret to being happy was, and you hugged me. That was so nice of you. I know how many times you have brightened my day and I'm sure thousands of others. I made this crabapple jelly last night and wanted you to have some to let you know 'thank you' for your kindness. It is appreciated more than you will ever know."

I put the card back in the envelope and asked Marty who she was. He didn't know.

"This is what I'm talking about," Marty said. "When you are nice to people you get it all back and then some. Boy, do I feel good!"

CHAPTER SIX
Doing a Little More

∞ I asked Marty, "Is the customer always right?"

He replied quickly. "You bet they're always right." Then he thought about it. "Well," he said, "they're not always right. I don't tell them that. I listen to them. I might not agree with them, but I listen. They eventually wind down. I listen."

He said the word "listen" three times in answering the question. That's a lot of listening, I thought. Then I remembered the first time I met Marty. I was surprised he was actually listening to the customers as they were going through his line.

One person Marty listened to was Linda. In her early fifties, she always came through his line with a big smile. One day Marty noticed the smile had disappeared.

"Something was wrong. I knew it. So I asked her if she was okay," Marty said.

Linda told Marty she needed a heart transplant and was going to the University of Minnesota right away for surgery. She was frightened. Marty said, "I hugged her and told her everything was going to be all right."

Three months later Linda walked into the store, a new heart pumping in her chest. Marty said, "I got so excited I kissed her."

Not long after Marty told me the story I picked up our hometown newspaper and on the front page was a photograph of two women. A story accompanying the picture told readers that one woman needed a heart transplant and the other woman had survived that surgery. Her name was Linda Girard.

I didn't know Linda's last name until I read that story. Looking through the phone book, I found Linda's number and called her. "Linda," I said, "I'm a friend of Marty's."

Before I could say another word she replied, "You, too?"

"How often do you and Marty get together?" I asked.

"We don't get together," she said. "I see him at Wal-Mart."

"Well," I said, "the way he talks about you made me think you were good friends."

"We are good friends, but the only time I see him is at Wal-Mart," she said. "When I got home from my surgery there was a card sitting on the kitchen table. I looked at the return address and it read 'Aaron Martinson.' I didn't have a clue who Aaron Martinson was. I opened the card and it was signed 'your friend Marty at Wal-Mart.' So, to answer your question, yes, we are good friends."

I asked Marty why he sent her a card. "I just think if you want to be a friend," he replied, "sometimes you need to do a little more."

That was Marty's second lesson: *Try to do a little more.*

∞ Sometimes that philosophy ran contrary to company policy.

Cashiers were instructed never to put their own money into the register if a customer didn't have enough to pay a bill. Marty ignored this rule. "I've done it hundreds of times," he said.

If someone came up a few cents short in paying the bill, Marty would stick his hand in his pocket, grab a handful of change, and pay the difference. Pennies, nickels, dimes, and quarters were constantly going out of his pocket and into the cash drawer.

At times, though, the overage required more than pocket change. There was the case of a local minister's wife. She found herself twenty dollars short in paying her bill. Marty paid it. The next time she was back in Marty's line, she announced to the other customers, "This is the man who gave me twenty dollars!"

I asked him, "What's the most money you ever put in the till when someone was short?"

"Fifty-one dollars. I had to reach for my wallet on that one."

"Why do you do that?"

He thought for a moment. "Sometimes after I tell a customer how much they owe, they'll look in their wallets or purses and discover they don't have their money with them. They're embarrassed and I don't want to embarrass them in front of other customers by making them put stuff back. So, I take the money out of my pocket or wallet and throw it in the till. They always pay me back."

"Do they? Always?"

"One time I gave a guy ten dollars and he never paid me back," Marty said. He paused and then smiled. "I know he feels worse than I do."

⁂ People knew Marty was genuine, and they gravitated to him.

He told me about two different women who appeared in his line at various times but bought nothing. He guessed that they were lonely or had personal troubles. They stood in his line for one thing: a hug. He would hug them and say a few kind words, and they would simply disappear.

"Maybe they felt nobody appreciated them," he said. "I just wanted them to know I did."

After watching Marty hug one of the women, a man standing in his line asked, "Are you some kind of preacher?"

Marty answered, "I just want to be a friend."

He also cast no judgments on the people who went through his line. Maybe it stemmed from his childhood. Everyone was treated with respect, regardless of how they looked or what they bought.

Every August in South Dakota, there is a big motorcycle rally held in the town of Sturgis at the foot of the beautiful Black Hills. Many bikers travel through our town on the way to the rally. Some of those visitors stop at stores along the highway.

A few years ago, when the rally was about to begin, I was standing in Marty's line, right behind a biker. He was big and wore a lot of leather, his arms were filled with tattoos, and his hair was in a pony tail. I kept my distance.

Marty treated the biker like he was the mayor of our town. "You be safe," Marty told the guy. The biker walked out of the store with a huge smile on his face. Marty, serving as an unofficial ambassador for our chamber of commerce, made him feel welcome and appreciated. I wouldn't have been as kind.

I had made a value judgment about the biker. Marty did not. Sometimes doing a little more means placing greater emphasis on human decency.

∮ I admired Marty for many reasons, but how he treated children won all the blue ribbons. At most stores, kids are looked upon as a necessary nuisance. They don't have much buying power and come up short on the customer treatment scale.

"Kids just love it when I shake their hands. Future customers, you know," Marty said with a wink.

A couple of days before Father's Day, a little girl in line with her mother walked up to Marty and handed him an envelope. He opened it and found a Father's Day card. The little girl signed her name and included her picture.

Marty couldn't speak. Realizing his predicament, the mother explained. "It was my daughter's idea. She insisted we buy you a card because you are so nice to her whenever she goes through your line. She thinks you must be a terrific father to somebody."

One night I met Marty and Mickey at the Chinese restaurant. We ordered the buffet and got up from our table to fill our plates. Marty went to one side of the buffet line, Mickey and I went down the other.

Just then, a little boy, maybe five years old, walked past Marty. The boy stopped dead in his tracks and stared at Marty. Then he turned to all of the people seated in the restaurant and shouted, "Mom … Dad

…. it's Marty from Wal-Mart!"

Mickey ducked her head as if to hide. "See," she said, "we can't go anywhere anymore."

We finished filling our plates and sat down at our table, Mickey near the window and Marty across from me. A while later the little boy came running toward us. Five feet from the table he leaped. He intended to land on Marty's lap, but he came up about a foot short.

The boy bounced off the table and fell on the floor—but not before sending Marty's plate into the air. The food went flying. Stunned, I didn't know what to do.

Marty did. He got out of his chair, picked the little boy off the ground and sat him on his lap.

After having worked all day, Marty was tired and hungry. Yet there he sat, with wet egg noodle on his shirt, and he listened to everything that little boy said to him. I stopped eating and watched all of this in silence. After about five minutes, the child's mother and father appeared at our table to collect their son.

The boy jumped off Marty's lap. Marty stood and shook the hands of the mother and father. Then the family left the restaurant.

"Marty," I asked, "who was that?"

"Some people who go through my line at Wal-Mart."

Mickey told me what Marty didn't. "The little boy just lost his grandpa," she said. "He asked Marty to be his grandpa now."

Sometimes you need to do a little more.

"I just want to be a friend."

CHAPTER SEVEN
The Source of Happiness

∽ At times Marty made it sound too easy. On a visit to his home I heard him say, "People need to decide to be happy."

I pressed him. "What do you mean by that?"

His face took on an incredulous look. "You have to ask me?"

At that moment I felt a little foolish. Complex human problems, at least to me, often prevent people from being happy. To Marty it was a matter of common sense. I wondered, what was I missing?

"C'mon, Marty," I said, "do you really think people can actually decide to be happy?"

"Who makes decisions for you?" Marty asked me. "All my life I've watched people waiting for someone else to make them happy. The way I got it figured, the only one who can make you happy is you."

As I considered his point, my mind began to wander. Strangely, I thought of an old "Peanuts" cartoon—the one in which Lucy asked Charlie Brown, "Why do you think we were put on earth?"

Charlie Brown answered, "To make others happy."

"I don't think I'm making anyone happy," Lucy replied, "but nobody's making me very happy either." Then Lucy screamed out, "Somebody's not doing his job!"

I smiled at that moment, thinking Marty had something in common with Charles Schultz, the creator of the "Peanuts" cartoon. Both seemed to be saying that it was silly to expect other people to have such an influence over our lives.

That was Marty's third lesson: *Only you can make you happy.*

∞ That night Marty told me a story that was very personal for him. I knew Marty and Mickey had four children. I didn't know there had been a fifth. She was their second child, Lynette, born with spina bifida. She died shortly after birth.

Forty years later, Marty still grieved for her.

"The funeral director was a super guy," Marty said. "He knew we didn't have any money, but he told us he would take care of our little girl. He went out and built a wood casket for her and lined it with white satin."

Marty's voice started to break. "He only charged us five dollars. He knew we wanted to pay, but he only charged us five bucks.

"It's stuff like that. You can look for the good in people and you'll find the good. You can look for the bad in people and you'll find the bad. The way I've got it figured, you'll find what you are looking for. I'd just as soon look for the good in people."

I didn't know what it was like to grow up poor. I had never known the hardship of trying to live on a meager budget while raising a family.

Marty's life was filled with minimum-wage jobs, borrowing on insurance policies, and working overtime to make a little more money. When his father died, he inherited one thing: a Zippo lighter with a pheasant imprinted on it.

Even in the autumn of his life, Marty worked. He wanted the company's health benefits as much as the wages. Sure, he enjoyed his job, but he felt he needed to work. Before I met Marty he had suffered

a heart attack and prostate cancer. When he talked about these problems, though, it was to tell me about all the cards his fellow employees
had sent to him.

In my lifetime I had seen people in similar circumstances grow
angry. Bitterness took hold of their lives and choked them.

"I never had much money, and I don't think I ever will," Marty
said. "People think they need to have a lot of things to make them
happy. They ought to look around and see what's really important."

When Marty looked around, he saw the most beautiful girl in the
world as his wife, four children who loved him, a home he was proud
of, and a job that made him feel alive. He was happy because, in his
mind, he had it all.

"People need to decide to be happy."

CHAPTER EIGHT

It's A Wonderful Story

∞ After a week's vacation, I came home and played the messages on my answering machine. One was from Marty. "You'll never believe what they're doing with me," he said. "They're flying me to Dallas, Texas, this Friday. I guess I'm going to be getting some big award. I'll let you know about it when I get back." Click.

I was in Marty's line early that next Monday. When he looked up from his cash register and saw me, he walked around the counter and grabbed me by the elbow. "I don't want to sound like a braggart, but you have got to come over tonight. You won't believe it. I don't believe it. Can you come over?"

I had never seen Marty that excited. Shortly after I arrived at his home that evening, he ushered me into the kitchen. "Look at this," he said, showing me a certificate. "It's Wal-Mart's Hero Award. They give out six of these a year."

Over the next hour Marty told me all about the award and his trip to Dallas. He received the honor in front of thirteen thousand managers and supervisors of the largest company in the world. "They told me only one in a hundred thousand associates gets the award," he said. "Pretty good, huh?"

The speaker that day was General Colin Powell. Marty said, "I was maybe ten feet from him when he spoke. He's a powerful speaker. I don't have a clue what he was talking about, but he looked at me the whole time."

The certificate wasn't the only new source of pride in Marty's home. While he was in Texas, his children went through family albums and picked out photographs taken of Marty during important times of his life. They had the pictures matted and placed in a large frame that now was hanging in the dining room.

Marty took me over to the new wall hanging. I immediately got a lump in my throat. There, mixed in with all those pictures of Marty, was a copy of the letter I had sent to David Glass, president and CEO of Wal-Mart, all those months ago.

I looked at Marty. He knew I was focused on my letter. "You know," he said, "I've read your letter seventy-five times, and I've cried seventy-five times."

∞ I couldn't sleep that night. Over and over I replayed that moment. Contentment had filled Marty's face. He seemed like he was the richest man in town.

"That's it!" I shouted. I jumped out of bed and grabbed my notebook. It had finally dawned on me that Marty was a modern-day George Bailey, the character Jimmy Stewart played in the Christmas movie, *It's a Wonderful Life.*

George Bailey never got to travel the world, never became a builder of great cities, and never made a lot of money. It wasn't until he saw the world without him, courtesy of Angel Second Class Clarence Oddbody, that he realized the impact of his life on others.

At the end of the movie, Harry Bailey, George's younger brother, raised a glass in the air and said, "Here's a toast to my big brother, George, the richest man in town."

In my mind, Marty was the richest man in our town. So many people were being touched by his kindness, if only for a moment. He reminded all of us to be better people.

I wanted the whole world to know about him—or at least as many people as my voice could reach. For the next few months I worked on a speech titled, "The Richest Man in Town." I knew how he was affecting my life, and I felt other people needed to hear his story.

Several weeks later, I tried out the talk in front of two hundred people. The impact was immediate and powerful. I could see it in the faces of those sitting in the audience. When I was done, there was a standing ovation. I knew they weren't standing for me—they were standing for Marty.

Dozens of people came up to me afterwards, visibly moved by what they had heard, and thanked me. For some of them, Marty brought up memories of an important person in their lives and they wanted to tell me about that person.

"Thank you for reminding me how to be a better person," one man said.

"No," I replied, "you need to thank Marty."

CHAPTER NINE
Road Trip

∞ I had two speeches to deliver one Saturday, in South Dakota cities separated by two hundred miles. The first stop would be Dell Rapids to speak to a Lions convention. Then on to Pierre, the state capital, for a chamber of commerce event.

It would be a long day, but both Marty and Mickey wanted to go with me. As we drove out of our town, Mickey leaned forward from the back seat and asked, "Honey, did you bring a handkerchief?"

"I brought three," Marty said. "One for Dell Rapids, one for Pierre, and one for regular use."

Marty always cried during my talks. From start to finish, tears would roll down his cheeks. I think he was overwhelmed with the idea that someone was standing in front of hundreds of people talking about his life. He couldn't believe it, even after listening to me talk dozens of times.

The first time he came to listen, I caught a glimpse of his face and almost broke down myself. After that we struck a deal. He could sit off to the side but not in front of me while I spoke. We were both better off that way.

∞ Marty and Mickey had lived in Dell Rapids shortly after they were married. He was excited at the thought of seeing old friends. Not long after arriving at the high school gymnasium, the site of the convention, he spotted a woman named Norma. She and her husband had owned the newspaper when Marty worked there.

Norma sat with Marty and Mickey as I gave a forty-five-minute talk to a crowd of one hundred seventy-five people. I concluded my remarks by introducing Marty. The entire audience stood and gave him a prolonged ovation.

Marty waved and smiled. Deep down he was proud to come back to Dell Rapids and be received in such a fashion. He would never say it, but I knew.

A photographer lined us up for a picture to appear in the town newspaper. But Marty wouldn't smile, not even when the photographer asked. He looked at me and said, "I have a stupid smile. One side of my mouth droops." After some prodding, Marty made a half-hearted attempt at smiling.

On the road to our next appearance, Marty remarked in passing, "I've never been to Pierre in my life." I couldn't believe it. He had lived in South Dakota for more than seventy years and had never been to the state capital. "Too busy working," he told me.

As we came into town, Marty asked, "Can we stop at the World War II Memorial? I'd really like to see it." I decided to go there before checking into the hotel.

The South Dakota World War II Memorial rests on a manmade peninsula, jutting out into a small body of water aptly named Capitol Lake. Geese and ducks winter there as warm artesian water prevents it from freezing. The lake lies less than three hundred feet from the State Capitol. At just the right angle, you can see the reflection of that grand building on the water's surface. It's a beautiful place and a perfect spot to honor veterans.

Marty walked around the memorial in silence. He surveyed the six life-size bronze statues, each one representing a different branch of the military. Pausing in front of the statue of a soldier, Marty asked, "Can you take my picture here?"

I didn't have to ask why. Nor did I ask him to smile for the picture. His solemn face reminded me of the night he told me he had watched so many of his friends die.

After a few more minutes, Marty said, "That's enough." We walked back to my car without saying a word to each other. He still didn't want to talk about the war. It was just something he kept deep inside him.

We checked into the hotel and got ready for the dinner. The woman in charge of the event told me they expected four hundred guests for the banquet. Speaking to that many people usually didn't bother me. On that night I was nervous. I'd never spoken to an audience filled with farmers and ranchers. Would they like the message? Would they think it was too corny?

On our way to the banquet hall we passed by the coat racks. Dozens of black cowboy hats, all resting upside down, filled the top rows. That sight brought my anxiety to a fever pitch. I was so nervous

I couldn't eat. Instead, I walked around until I was finally introduced and then walked onto the stage.

The crowd was attentive and engaging. With each passing minute I felt more comfortable. You could have heard a pin drop in that room while I spoke. They were getting it—and getting Marty.

My talk was nearly over when I said, "Marty had never been to Pierre in his life—until today." There was an audible gasp from the audience. "Marty," I asked, "would you stand up?"

Before he could get to his feet, all four hundred people in the room were on theirs. People couldn't see Marty so I motioned him to come up onto the stage. He walked up the steps, we hugged, and I left him on the stage alone. For a full two minutes the audience stood and clapped. Marty lowered his head and cried.

It was the greatest moment of my speaking life.

Immediately after the master of ceremonies ended the night's activities, a long line of people formed to see Marty. Some wanted to shake his hand, others wanted a hug. Two people wanted autographs.

The next morning we drove out of Pierre and headed for home. Marty said, "I couldn't get to sleep last night. I was so excited."

I couldn't sleep, either.

CHAPTER TEN
Celebrity Status

∞ "All this started because you wrote that letter," Marty would say.

"No," I would reply, "all this started because of your kindness." It was an argument that neither of us could win.

I was giving my speech "The Richest Man in Town" forty to fifty times a year. In small towns, big business meetings, high school graduations, and at the base of Mount Rushmore, the message was always the same. The reaction from the crowds was always the same, too. Those who heard it wondered, is Marty for real?

Many people had to find out for themselves. People would come to the Wal-Mart in our town after they had heard me speak about him. Some would be driving on Interstate 29, which passes just outside our town, and decide to make a detour just to see if he was really there, wearing his red vest, ringing up purchases, shaking hands and giving hugs.

Two men drove one hundred fifty miles out of their way to meet him. A group of women who had heard me speak at a convention in a distant city decided to make a special trip to see him. At this Marty said, "I must be getting pretty popular."

Mickey was sitting next to Marty at the kitchen table when he told me about the women visiting him. She brushed his hand and said, "Don't you start getting a big head!"

Marty laughed. "I know, I know. Just when you start to think you're somebody, something happens to put you in your place."

That had happened to Marty a few days earlier at a grocery store. A guy walked up to him and said, "Boy, I haven't seen you since they closed down K-Mart."

∞ True, Marty had gained some measure of fame from my talks in distant places. Around our hometown and for the people in the area, he didn't need the publicity. Every person who went through his line remembered him.

South Dakota's largest paper, the Argus Leader in Sioux Falls, published a story about Marty in the Thanksgiving edition. College students, as part of their classroom assignments on customer service, would drop by and videotape Marty as he performed his magic at his checkout counter.

Ministers talked about him in their Sunday sermons. Customers would come by the store on Monday and say, "I heard about you at church yesterday, Marty. The preacher said we need to be more like you." Marty would blush, not quite knowing what to say. It was all very heady stuff.

One fall I received a call from a very excited Marty. "Guess what I've been asked to do?" A group of people from the local chamber of commerce had stopped at the store and asked him to serve as the grand marshal for the Festival of Lights Parade, which ushers in the Christmas season. It's an honor usually reserved for local dignitaries and political types. "Why do you think they chose me?" Marty asked. He still didn't get it.

∽ The temperature was ten degrees on the night of the parade. Steam rose from anything even remotely warm—an idling car, the tops of buildings, the mouths and nostrils of passers-by. A strong wind from the north whipped away those little clouds and made the darkness feel even colder.

I joined a group of people huddled in front of our post office. Ten minutes before the parade was to begin, the sidewalks were empty. I felt sorry for Marty. It was a big moment in his life and the weather wasn't cooperating.

All that changed when a police car's siren signaled the start of the parade. People got out of their cozy cars and left the comfort of shops and stores. Curbsides were soon filled with children and other people bundled up in their warm coats. "Look, Mom!" one little girl shouted. "Here they come!"

A color guard led the parade. Everyone on both sides of the street placed their glove-covered right hands over their hearts as the American flag passed by. Then came the moment I was waiting for—the vehicle carrying the grand marshal came gliding down the street.

Marty and Mickey were in the back seat of a pickup truck with an extended cab. Both were wearing Santa Claus hats. Sitting on the left side with his window rolled down, Marty waved furiously at the crowd.

I broke from the crowd and walked toward the pickup truck. The woman who was driving the truck smiled when she saw me and brought the vehicle to a stop. I stuck my hand inside the window to shake Marty's hand. I said, "I'm proud of you."

Marty had an enormous smile on his face. "Isn't this something!" he exclaimed.

I walked back to my place in the crowd. For the next few minutes I watched as the pickup truck moved slowly down the street. Marty's hand protruded from the half-opened window, never ceasing to wave the entire time I watched. People in the crowd waved back. Some yelled, "Yea, Marty!"

A young woman from the chamber of commerce told me they had received many calls from people thanking them for choosing Marty. He sent the office a card thanking its members for making him grand marshal. "We all remember him for that," the woman said. Marty had been such a hit with everyone that the chamber planned to ask him to be grand marshal again.

Fate had a different idea.

CHAPTER ELEVEN
Saying Good-bye

❧ Marty and I were sitting at his kitchen table when he asked me for a favor. "I want you to give the eulogy at my funeral."

We had never talked about death. "Well …," I said, fumbling for the right words.

Marty wasn't going to let me squirm. "Mick and I sat down with the funeral director today and did some pre-planning. We didn't think it was fair to leave that stuff up to the kids. So we decided to take care of things early just in case something happened. Will you do it?"

I stuttered a bit, but then the right words came to me. "Sure, Marty. I'd be proud to give your eulogy. It's probably going to be pretty long, though."

He winked at me and replied, "You take all the time you need."

∽ It was Marty who didn't have enough time.

A little over two months later Marty found himself in the hospital. For more than a year he had been losing weight, and doctors couldn't figure out why. His white blood cell count was low and he was advised to quit work. White blood cells fight infection, and doctors feared he might fall victim to a disease passed along by a customer.

If he couldn't quit working, one doctor suggested, he might consider wearing a mask and stop shaking hands with customers. Marty wouldn't even consider it. "Now, that would kill me. I won't do it," he said.

Marty continued to shake hands—and he continued losing weight. Something was wrong.

A diagnosis finally came: an infected gall bladder. Now Marty faced the decision of surgery. "Well," he said, "I can't go on like this."

Mickey called me after her husband had left the operating room. The surgery had taken far longer than expected because the infection had spread beyond the gall bladder. "He's a mess inside," she said.

Marty was in for the fight of his life.

I decided not to visit Marty for a few days. He needed rest, and the drugs for the pain made him a little incoherent. He was dropping in and out of consciousness.

I had to summon a bit of courage to drive to the hospital, even more to find my way to the intensive care unit. A nurse told me I needed to wear a gown, mask, and plastic gloves. While putting on those protective garments I worried about what my friend would look like lying in the hospital bed. Was he in pain? How many hoses did he have connected to him? Would he even recognize me? All these thoughts had me on edge as I approached the room where they told me Marty lay.

Inside the room, I drew back a white curtain and saw a man lying on his back. He was sleeping. As I moved closer I could see a small hose leading from his nose and disappearing off the side of the bed. His mouth was wide open, sucking in as much air as his lungs could handle. I looked down at a face I didn't recognize.

I quickly retreated from this stranger's room. I went to the nurse's station and asked the young woman behind the desk if she could tell me where I could find Aaron Martinson. She pointed to the room I had just left.

At that moment I wanted to rip off the gown, throw aside the mask and gloves, and go home as fast as I could. But I knew that my friend needed me—and I needed him.

Slowly, I walked up to the side of Marty's bed. I stood there for a few minutes, staring at him and feeling sorry for him. On the other side of his bed, various pieces of hospital equipment were flashing lights and numbers. All of these things were connected to Marty, and I didn't know what they meant.

Then Marty's eyes opened. He looked at me and lifted his left hand off the bed. It was a sign he wanted me to grab his hand, which I did. He whispered, "Hi, buddy."

"How are you feeling?" I asked.

"It hurts," he said. Then, he drifted off to sleep.

Soon, a young woman walked into the room. A physical therapist, she woke Marty and told him she needed to move his legs and asked for his help. He groaned at the thought. Before she began, she asked Marty, "Is this your friend?" and nodded in my direction.

Marty said, "Yes, his name is V.J. Smith."

"Is he a good friend?"

Marty answered, "Don't get me started."

∞ The pain eventually went away, but Marty never got better. He lingered in the hospital for five weeks. His body slowly began to shut down. His spirit, too.

I tried to think of ways to make Marty want to live. I didn't need to remind him that customers were waiting for him to return to Wal-Mart. More than four hundred get-well cards flooded his room. Some were from people Marty knew only by what they bought. One was signed "The Cat Food Man" and another simply "The Tomato Lady."

On one of my visits I suggested we read some of the cards. After I had read just two of them aloud, Marty said, "That's enough for now." It bothered me because Marty had always enjoyed receiving notes from people.

"I suppose if I die you will have to stop talking about me," Marty said.

I replied, "Marty, as long as I'm around people are going to hear all about you."

He smiled. He wanted to be remembered.

∞ On a later visit, Marty shared something with me that, to this day, I can't quite comprehend. "I know when Mickey is in the hospital coming to visit me," he told me. "I feel her presence. Five minutes before she comes in my room, I know she's here. Isn't that strange?"

I didn't quite know what to say to him, so I just smiled.

Mickey was on his mind. "Promise me something," he said. "If I die, don't forget Mickey. I'd appreciate it if you would still visit her." I promised him I would do that.

A half-hour later, Marty looked at me and said, "Mick's here." Five minutes later the door to his room opened and Mickey walked in.

I didn't want to think about how difficult Marty's illness was for Mickey. Once, when I was visiting, Mickey said she needed to go home. Still wearing the mask that protected Marty from germs, she bent down to kiss him good-bye. He said, "Take that damned thing off!"

Mickey said she couldn't. He held her close for a moment, then said, "You have beautiful eyes."

∞ Marty seemed to be shrinking before our eyes. One day I stopped by the Martinson home and found Mickey crying. She said, "They've given up on him." I asked her what she meant. The doctors no longer required visitors to wear masks.

I knew I needed to make what might be my last visit. I stopped outside Marty's room when I heard someone talking to him. It was a doctor telling Marty his kidneys had shut down and he needed dialysis. Marty said nothing and the doctor left.

I walked in and sat down on a chair near his bed. He wasn't wearing his glasses, so I asked him if he could see okay. He whispered, "I see well enough to see my friend."

I turned away, not wanting Marty to see the tears running down my face. After a moment, I looked back at him and he raised his right hand. I grabbed it and held it tight.

Marty said, "I'm sorry I'm cutting our friendship short. I wished I'd met you a long time ago."

For the next twenty minutes I held Marty's hand. He would drift in and out of consciousness, saying a few words before falling back to sleep. His eyes looked cloudy, yet he seemed focused on some distant place. His face bore no expression. He seemed very much at peace.

It was time to say our final good-bye. I stood up, bent down close to his face, and said, "I love you, Marty." He locked onto my eyes and replied, "I love you, too."

These were the last words we spoke to each other.

Early the next morning, I received a call from Marty's daughter, Lori. She said her father had taken a turn for the worse during the night. Two days later, he died.

More than four hundred get-well cards
flooded his room.

CHAPTER TWELVE
A Time to Mourn

∞ A profound sense of sadness shrouded the Martinson home. I dropped by to visit, only hours after Marty had died. Mickey and I hugged each other, and our bodies shook with grief.

Holding her, I whispered, "I'm sorry, Mick."

She said, "I know."

I followed Mickey into the kitchen and we sat down at the table where Marty had taught me so much. Members of their family moved about, not quite knowing what to do.

"We were thinking," Mickey said, "maybe Marty should wear his red Wal-Mart vest in the coffin. That's how most people remember him. What do you think?"

In that instant I couldn't think. I began to cry. Mickey handed me a tissue. In my head I could see him lying there, lifeless, yet strangely proud. My mind's eye seemed to focus on one thing: the name tag bearing "Marty" in bold letters. It would be the same badge I had seen the first time I met him. The thought of Marty's body wearing that vest was so sad, yet so very right.

The funeral was set for a Friday morning at a church in our town. The family assembled in the church basement a half-hour before the service. I was asked to join them as I was to give the eulogy I had promised Marty four months earlier.

"It's time," the funeral director told us. We marched up the steps and followed Marty's coffin, now covered with an American flag, into the worship hall. The church was so filled with people I couldn't pick out any one person.

All had filed past the coffin. He appeared as so many would remember him, wearing the red Wal-Mart vest, the name tag "Marty" pinned on the breast. Then the coffin was closed and, draped with an American flag, brought to the front of the hall.

There was a song, some readings, and another song. The next thing I knew I was standing at the pulpit talking about my friend. I took Marty's advice and took all the time I needed, filling the eulogy with his favorite stories. There was laughter and some tears.

I read from some of the cards sent to Marty when he was in the hospital. I felt it was important to share what other people thought of him.

One woman wrote: "Heard you were not feeling well. I'm praying for you and hoping you will recover soon. I enclosed a photo of myself with my husband and family, as I was not sure you would remember me by name but thought you would remember the face. I've moved to Wisconsin now but remember your warmth and consider you one of those special people I shall never forget. God made you special, Marty, with a heart twice as big as most folks and I love you for it."

To me, Marty represented everything a person of God should be.

After the pastor spoke, two members of the local American Legion Post, dressed in ceremonial attire, took positions at each end of the coffin. They carefully lifted the American flag off the coffin and slowly folded it into a neat triangle. The group leader, now holding the folded flag, walked toward the Martinson family.

Mickey and the family stood up. The leader presented the flag to

Mickey and said, "On behalf of the president of the United States and the people of a grateful nation, may I present this flag as a token of appreciation for the honorable and faithful service your loved one rendered this nation." I could hear people weeping.

The funeral director, another one of Marty's friends, had suggested a beautiful tribute for the conclusion of the service. A handshake had been Marty's signature to the world. So Marty's coffin was rolled to the entrance way of the worship hall. As people filed by, they placed a hand on the coffin, the gesture a final handshake for a friend.

∞ Anyone in our town who had not heard about Marty's death would have learned about it by reading our local newspaper. The obituary in its pages captured his spirit—and probably would have made him blush.

"Marty left an indelible mark on the many people who passed through his line at Wal-Mart," the newspaper observed. "No one was a stranger in his line, merely a friend in waiting. His life, guided by his positive attitude, was an inspiration to many people. Saddened by the loss of a husband, father, and friend, people take comfort knowing that Heaven has found a new greeter."

That weekend I found myself drawn to Wal-Mart. There was an eerie emptiness when I walked in the store. But I had heard that Marty's co-workers did something special in honor of him and I needed to see it.

Aisle 9 had been Marty's cash register. It was now decorated with balloons, flowers, pictures of Marty, candles, and a bowl of candy. The light above the cash register was on, signifying that Marty was at his post. Large sheets of poster board lay on the counter for people to write personal thoughts to Marty and his family.

From a safe distance I watched the shoppers as they stopped to pay their respects. Many stood silently, stared at the pictures, and wiped tears from their eyes. I recognized a woman who lived in another town. She was visibly moved, and I stepped forward to ask her if she was all right. "I only saw him once a month for just a few minutes," she said while crying. "He was such a sweet man."

A young woman, with brightly dyed red hair, spent five minutes looking at the pictures and reading some of the notes people had left. Then she gathered her things and went through a checkout line. She had walked twenty feet toward the exit before she stopped and put her bags on the ground. She went back to aisle 9 and wrote a note, not able to leave without saying good-bye.

Hundreds of people did this. "Thank you for making me smile," wrote Christine. A man named Bob wrote, "Marty, you were always so nice to me and my mother." Sheryl penned, "We always went out of our way to stand in Marty's line. He made our day." A woman by the name of Sharon wrote, "We need more Marty's in this world."

Yes, Sharon, we certainly do.

No one was a stranger in his line,
merely a friend in waiting.

CHAPTER THIRTEEN
Those Precious Few Moments

∞ Few people can actually change the world. Marty showed me that *you* can change *your* world. Along the way, you have the opportunity to be a powerful influence on the lives of other people, no matter your position in life.

It became clear to me when I visited the small town of Tracy, Minnesota, on a Sunday morning, eight months after Marty had died. I gave the sermon at a Lutheran church in that farming community. It was my third trip to Tracy in less than five months. I had talked about Marty in front of the entire teaching staff just before the start of school.

Three weeks later, I received a phone call from the elementary school principal. The grade school teachers wanted to make Marty the central character in their "Character Counts" program. I smiled at the notion. Marty would have smiled, too.

Officials planned a kick-off for the program for early October. I jumped at the opportunity to speak to the children about Marty's life. Then I called Mickey to see if she would come with me. She didn't hesitate, not even for a moment.

We stood alone in the small school gymnasium that October morning. An announcement over the loudspeaker reminded everyone that the program was about to begin. Soon, more than three hundred children, many with cherubic faces, were sitting on the floor of the gym waiting for me to speak.

For the next fifteen minutes I talked about my friend. The kids listened, which surprised me. Anyone with children knows it's difficult to keep their attention, but they listened. At the end of my talk I introduced Mickey. The children clapped.

Some children stepped forward to remove a large piece of paper that covered a bulletin board. Exposed, the board read "Marty Says" and listed the lessons he had shared with me while we sat at the kitchen table of Number Fifty-seven Normandy Village.

The music teacher came forward, reminded the children to sing loud, and then led those three hundred voices in a rousing rendition of a song from the musical *Scrooge*, singing, "Thank you very much! Thank you very much! That's the nicest thing that anyone's ever done for me!"

At the conclusion of the program, the children stood in a long line in front of Mickey. Each child hugged her. A nine-year-old boy said, "I'm sorry you lost your husband." Tears fell from Mickey's eyes—mine, too.

A few days after our trip to Tracy, I received an envelope containing letters from students in the fifth grade. One young girl wrote: "I want to thank you for coming to talk to us about your good friend Marty. Now I feel like Marty is my friend, too. You gave a very good speech. It touched everyone's heart forever. I knew after your speech that I wanted to be just like Marty."

Those words were on my mind as I prepared to give the sermon at the Tracy Lutheran Church a few months later. Marty, a simple man who ran a cash register, had touched her life.

As I sat in the pew, listening to the choir, I couldn't help but

THE RICHEST MAN IN TOWN

marvel at all that had happened since I had met Marty. The nights at the kitchen table, the countless speeches to thousands of people. Now, I was sitting in a church, ready to tell his story again—and to share with others what guided Marty's life.

Relationships matter most in life.

Try to do a little more.

Only you can make you happy.

Marty had died, but his goodness still lived. I'm convinced that people constantly seek reminders of kindness. In Marty, people take a personal inventory of their own lives to reflect on their relationships. Marty gets in their heads.

On many occasions I've received notes from people who said that, after listening to one of my talks, they have called their mothers or fathers to thank them for all they have done. The reaction from the parents is always the same: They wonder what's wrong. The unexpected gratitude blindsides them. Then, tears of joy flow, all tapped by a simple reminder of kindness.

A local radio station broadcast the sermon that Sunday. A few days after the talk, the pastor wrote to tell me about a man who was listening while driving down a highway. He had to pull over to the side of the road because he was weeping. He had been forced to give thought to the relationships in his life.

Marty's greatest lesson was not what he told me but what he constantly showed me. In one or two minutes of time we have the opportunity to define ourselves as human beings. There isn't much room for error.

Two minutes is what Marty spent with most customers. If you think about it, two minutes is about the average amount of time we spend with most people in our lives.

In a precious few moments, what we say and what we do can be lasting.

Want proof? Not long ago a young woman approached me after I had completed a talk. I was speaking in a town one hundred fifty miles from home. The woman was crying. She told me the last time she had seen Marty was four years earlier, while she was still a college student.

With tears in her eyes, she said, "He always made me feel like I was beautiful." Then we hugged. There was no need to say anything else.

Marty was in our heads.

About the Author

V.J. Smith grew up in the small town of Eureka, SD and his early life was shaped by a raucous household filled with three brothers and four sisters. He graduated from South Dakota State University and considers himself fortunate to have served as Executive Director of the SDSU Alumni Association.

A professional speaker for more than two decades, V.J. gives presentations to businesses, organizations and schools throughout the country. He is the author of two other books: *Can You Hear What I See?* and *Jackrabbit Tales*.

Visit his website at: *www.vj-smith.com*

You can contact V. J. via e-mail: *thankyou@brookings.net*

Acknowledgments

I would like to thank Mickey Martinson for sharing Marty with me. I'd like to thank my wife, Julie, and our children for their support. And, I'd like to thank Doug Daniel for his help in editing this book.

A middle school student in Delaware, Ohio taped this handcrafted image of Marty's badge onto a locker a day after I spoke there. The school secretary sent me the photo. Delaware is nine hundred forty one miles from Brookings, South Dakota. It's a lot to think about.